Belvedere
GR 2-5

EARTHQUAKES

Earth's Mightiest Moments

by **David L. Harrison**

Illustrated by **Cheryl Nathan**

Boyds Mills Press

The author wishes to thank Erwin J. Mantel, Ph.D, professor of geology, Southwest Missouri State University; and Michelle Barret and Diane M. Noserale, of the United States Geological Survey, for their assistance in developing this book.

Published by Boyds Mills Press, Inc.
A Highlights Company
815 Church Street
Honesdale, Pennsylvania 18431
Printed in China

Library of Congress Cataloging-in-Publication Data

Harrison, David L.
   Earthquakes : earths mightiest moments / by David L. Harrison ;
illustrated by Cheryl Nathan.— 1st ed.
p.   cm.
ISBN 1-59078-243-7 (alk. paper)
1. Earthquakes—Juvenile literature. [1. Earthquakes.] I. Nathan,
Cheryl, 1958 – ill. II. Title.

QE521.3.H25 2004
551.22—dc22

2003026790
First edition, 2004
The text of this book is set in 18-point Optima.

10 9 8 7 6 5 4 3 2 1

In Memory of John Harrison
   —D. L. H.

For the person who protected me through a real earthquake—
my mom, Florence
   —C. N.

In 1811, at two in the morning,
just nine days before Christmas,
settlers in New Madrid, Missouri,
were startled awake.
Their furniture was bouncing,
pots and pans flying.
Cabins shook.
Chimneys tumbled.
Roofs fell in.

Outside was worse.
Trees snapped in two.
The ground rolled.
Here and there its surface cracked
and squirted muddy water.
Rivers changed course.
People hundreds of miles away
felt the shocks.
At that time it was
the worst earthquake
in the history of the United States.

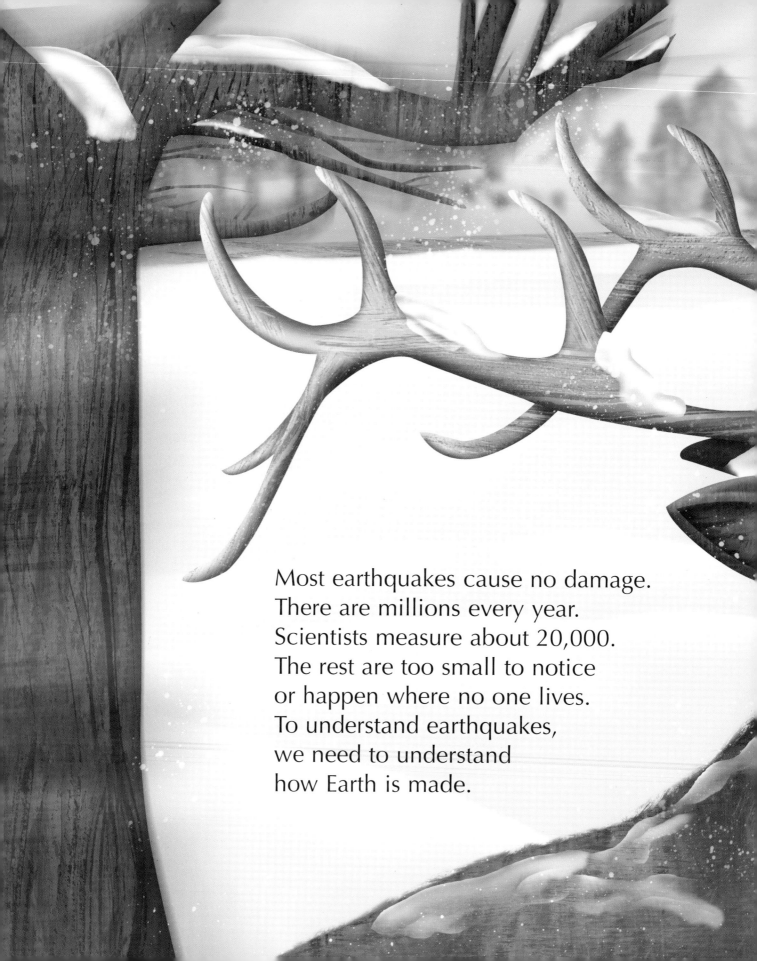

Most earthquakes cause no damage.
There are millions every year.
Scientists measure about 20,000.
The rest are too small to notice
or happen where no one lives.
To understand earthquakes,
we need to understand
how Earth is made.

Imagine a rock
up to sixty miles thick.
Imagine it bigger
than the United States.
Imagine it floating
on an ocean of rock
1,800 miles deep.

We call the rock a tectonic plate.
Scientists believe
that eight huge plates
and several smaller ones
cover the earth.

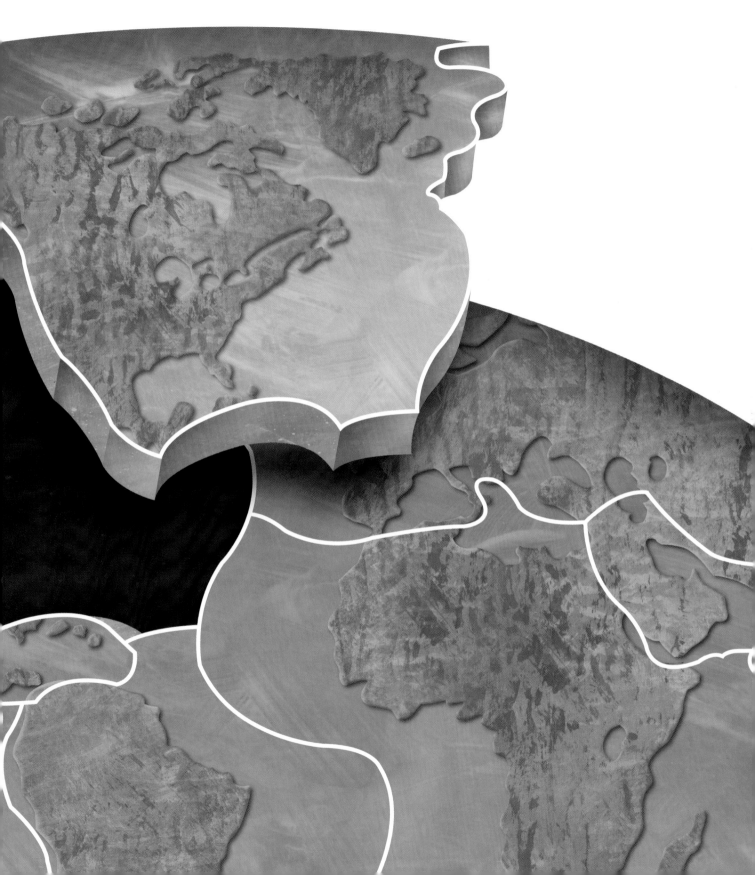

They form the crust,
the only part of our planet
cool enough to touch.
Oceans and mountains
and all the land
rest on the crust.
And so do we.

The core of Earth is mostly iron
that's hot enough to melt.
But it doesn't.
The great pressure of the world above
keeps it solid.

Around the center is an outer core.
Because pressure there is not as great,
rock in the outer core can melt.
Around the outer core is the mantle.
It is soft at the bottom where it's hottest,
and harder at the top near the crust.

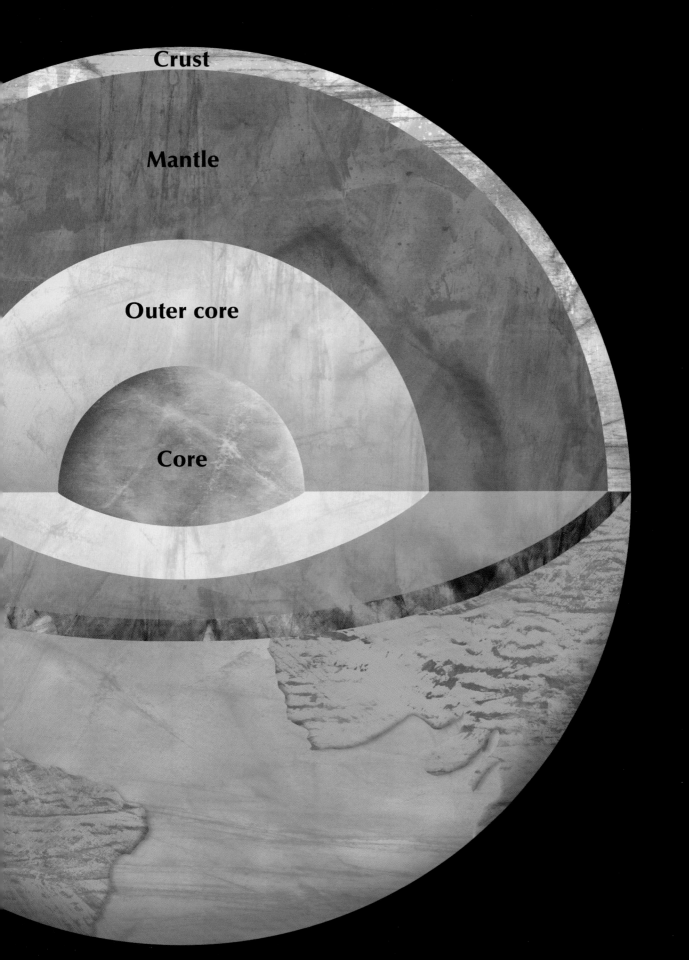

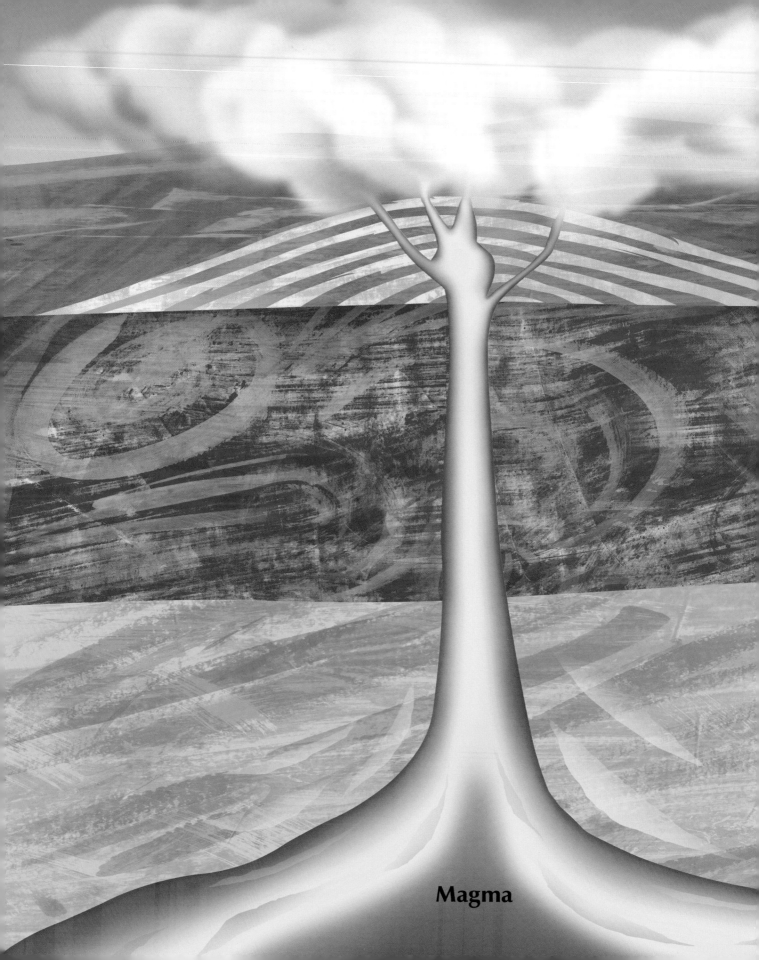

Magma

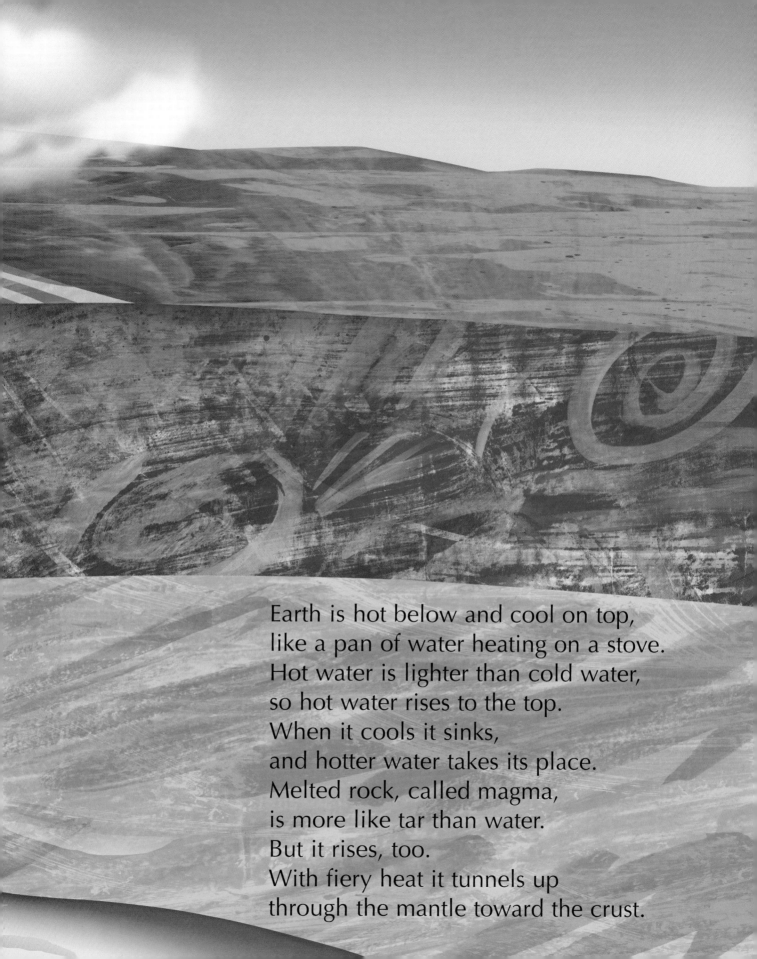

Earth is hot below and cool on top,
like a pan of water heating on a stove.
Hot water is lighter than cold water,
so hot water rises to the top.
When it cools it sinks,
and hotter water takes its place.
Melted rock, called magma,
is more like tar than water.
But it rises, too.
With fiery heat it tunnels up
through the mantle toward the crust.

Near the surface,
some magma cools into rock.
Some settles back down,
deeper in the mantle.
When magma escapes
through cracks in the crust,
we call it lava.

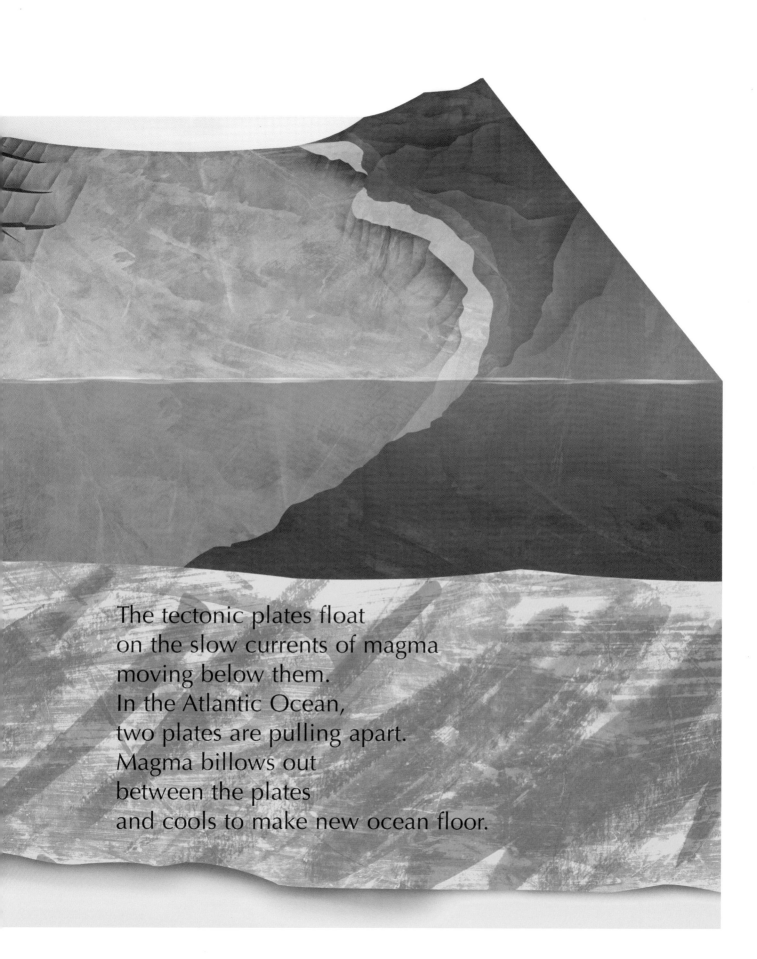

The tectonic plates float
on the slow currents of magma
moving below them.
In the Atlantic Ocean,
two plates are pulling apart.
Magma billows out
between the plates
and cools to make new ocean floor.

In the Pacific Ocean,
one plate slides over another.
The plates form a deep trench
thousands of miles long.
The edge of the plate on the bottom
is forced down into the mantle,
where it grows so hot it melts.

In California, two plates
rub against each other.
We call the line between them
the San Andreas Fault.
The stress causes rock below
to bend and fold until
sooner or later something breaks
and shakes the crust hard.

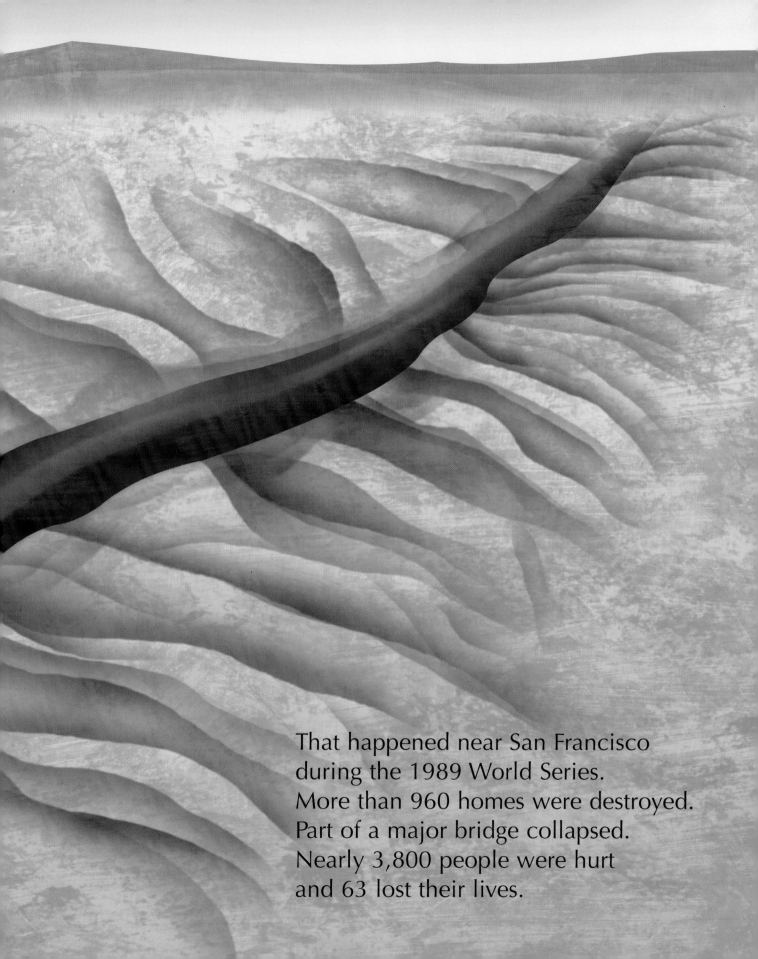

That happened near San Francisco
during the 1989 World Series.
More than 960 homes were destroyed.
Part of a major bridge collapsed.
Nearly 3,800 people were hurt
and 63 lost their lives.

When earthquakes that strong
happen under the ocean,
the shocks set off tsunami (soo-NAH-mee) waves.
These are waves
that speed across the water
and crash into shore.
Some tsunamis do more harm
than most earthquakes.

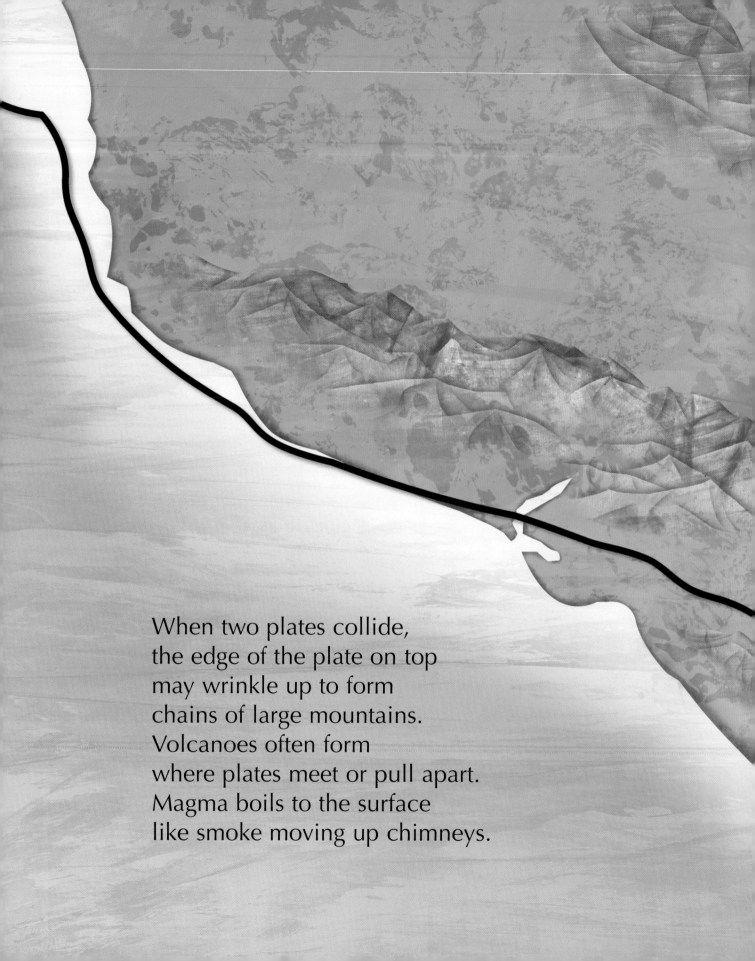

When two plates collide,
the edge of the plate on top
may wrinkle up to form
chains of large mountains.
Volcanoes often form
where plates meet or pull apart.
Magma boils to the surface
like smoke moving up chimneys.

But instead of smoke, it's melted rock
that pours from the ground.
If too much gas is trapped inside,
the eruption blows off
part of the mountain,
shooting chunks of lava
bigger than cars for miles.
Such powerful blasts
knock down forests
and send mud slides
roaring downhill,
burying everything below.

Scientists called seismologists
study earthquakes.
They measure strength of earthquakes
by giving them numbers called "magnitudes,"
often called Richter Scale magnitudes.
Each number is much stronger
than the one below it.
A 7 releases thirty-one times
more energy than a 6.
An 8 releases thirty-one times
more energy than a 7.
Worldwide, there may be one or two 8s in a year.
Most earthquakes measure only 1 or 2.
We know more now
than we did in 1811.
But Nature keeps many secrets.
We're still trying to discover
exactly when and where
Earth will have the next
of its mightiest moments.

AUTHOR'S NOTE

We struggle for ways to describe Earth's vast proportions. We compare tectonic plates to pieces of a jigsaw puzzle. Earth's circumference is more than 24,900 miles. The plates that cover its 197 million square miles vary from 3 miles thick to more than 60. Some jigsaw puzzle!

We say that the great rift running up the Atlantic Ocean floor resembles the seam on a baseball. The rift sprawls hundreds of miles wide and stretches over 40,000 miles. Along its length, tectonic plates are pulling apart. Lava storms boiling up through the cracks create jumbles of new crust sometimes topped by mountains a mile or more high. Some baseball!

And what we call plates are slabs of Earth's outer surface nearly too massive to comprehend. Imagine something carrying oceans and continents on its back while it is moving. Yet these behemoths do move. They shove, rub, or back away from one another, and their constant slow-motion traffic accidents keep Earth's outer crust in turmoil. Minor scrapes and snapping along plate edges cause millions of minor tremors every year. These do no harm, and most go unnoticed. But no force of nature can match the destructive energy released when major shifts occur in the outer surface of our planet.

This book provides young readers a first look at earthquakes and their causes. Later reading can explain in more detail how scientists piece together evidence on land and under the seas to learn more about Earth's mightiest moments. Here are other books on this subject recommended by librarians.

—David L. Harrison

FURTHER READING

Gentle, Victor, and Janet Perry. *Earthquakes*. Milwaukee, WI.: Gareth Stevens Publishing, 2001.
Lassieur, Allison. *Earthquake*. Mankato, MN.: Capstone Books, 2001.
McMorrow, Catherine. *Quakes!* New York: Random House, 2000.
Nicholson, Cynthia Pratt. *Earthquake!* New York: Kids Can Press Ltd., 2002.
Simon, Seymour. *Danger! Earthquakes*. New York: SeaStar Books, 2002.
Thompson, Luke. *Earthquakes*. New York: Children's Press, 2000.